GALORE PARK

So you really want to learn

Junior English
Book 1
Answer Book

Andrew Hammond MA

Series Editor: Susan Elkin MA BA(Hons) Cert Ed.

www.galorepark.co.uk

Published by Galore Park Publishing Ltd
19/21 Sayers Lane, Tenterden, Kent TN30 6BW
www.galorepark.co.uk

Text copyright © Andrew Hammond 2007

The right of Andrew Hammond to be identified as the author of this Work
has been asserted by him in accordance with sections 77 and 78 of the
Copyright, Designs and Patents Act 1998.

Typsetting by Typetechnique, London
Printed by Charlesworth Press, Wakefield

ISBN: 978 1 902984 87 2

All rights reserved: no part of this publication may be reproduced, stored in
a retrieval system, or transmitted in any form or by any means, electronic,
mechanical, photocopying, recording or otherwise, without either the prior
written permission of the copyright owner or a licence permitting restricted
copying issued by the Copyright Licensing Agency, Saffron House,
6-10 Kirby Street, London EC1N 8TS.

First published 2007, reprinted 2008, 2010, 2011

Details of other Galore Park publications are available at www.galorepark.co.uk

ISEB Revision Guides, publications and examination papers may also be
obtained from Galore Park.

Contents

Introduction

The following book offers teachers and parents a range of recommended answers to the questions in *Junior English 1*.

In some cases an answer will be a definitive one – regurgitating literal information, writing a definition, or adding a prefix, for example – but there are many other instances when questions require more reflection and, as a result, answers will vary. This is good practice, for English at this level is not an exact science. Children need to be encouraged to reflect, consider and express opinions in response to what they have read. For such questions, suggested answers are offered here, but they do not need to be taken too literally, or followed too rigidly. The beauty (and the frustration!) of language learning is that there may be an infinite range of acceptable answers out there. If the children have articulated their views coherently, and supported what they have said with some direct reference to the passage, they must be rewarded.

When working through the questions with your class or child, encourage them to see how the meaning of a word or phrase is always inextricably linked to the context in which it appears – i.e. the sentence that surrounds it. There are many questions that ask for translations, or definitions, of words and phrases. In these cases particularly, it is important to encourage young readers to 'go back to the text' and see how the author has used the word or phrase in the specific context. This is good preparation for Common Entrance, which requires careful, and repeated, reading of passages to ascertain meanings, draw inferences and deductions and reach conclusions. To this end, line references are given throughout *Junior English 1*.

Likewise, the old adage, 'read the question carefully' applies, and one might add 'read the answer' too, for mistakes are often missed in the rush to reach the end of a comprehension exercise. Above all, the children need to move beyond a cursory glance at passages and accompanying questions if they are to avoid those tangential answers that can be so costly in examinations.

Comprehension tasks are most effective when they encourage readers to *think* about what they are reading and *communicate* their relevant responses in efficient and enlightening ways. I hope that *Junior English 1* and this accompanying answer book assist you in encouraging children to become thoughtful, confident and communicative students.

Good luck.

A.J.H.
July 2007

Chapter 1

Exercise 1.1

1. The author was on his way to fetch the cows in for milking when he saw the badger.
2. The badger was right in the middle of a big pasture.
3. (a) The badger did not take the slightest notice of the author. It just carried on snuffling about in the grass.

    (b) It did not seem at all frightened by this visitor.
4. The author thought the badger may be 'deaf or blind or both' because it had not seemed to noticed him at all.
5. The badger's reaction was very different when the author returned the next day: he and his friend charged at the author, 'with a volley of furious grunts'.
6. Answers may vary, for example:

    I think the badger returned to the same spot the next day to catch the author and see him off his patch!

    or I think the badger returned to the same spot to continue snuffling in the grass.
7. Possible definitions are:

    (a) *biffed:*   clobbered, punched, hit, struck

    (b) *nocturnal:*   of the night

    (c) *sett:*   a badger's burrow or underground home

    (d) *solitary:*   lone, single

Exercise 1.2

1. Badgers are similar to skunks as they have black and white markings.
2. You are most likely to find a bat in a cave or an attic during the daytime.
3. Most hedgehogs have thousands of thick spines covering their backs to protect them from predators.
4. You would know there were moles in your garden by the molehills they create when digging their tunnels.
5. Owls are particularly good at catching mice and rabbits, even at night, because they have sensitive hearing and large eyes (which give them good night vision).
6. Squirrels are able to feed during the cold winter months by burying supplies of seeds, like acorns, in the ground.
7. Answers will vary. Look for reasons to support their choices.

8.   Possible definitions are:
        (a) *shy:*   timid, withdrawn, easily frightened
        (b) *mammals:*   animals of a type that suckles its young
        (c) *predators:*   creatures that hunt, killing other animals for food
        (d) *gnaw:*   bite or chew steadily

Exercise 1.4

1.   The <u>author</u> met a <u>badger</u> in a <u>field</u>.
2.   The <u>badger</u> returned the next <u>day</u> with a <u>friend</u>.
3.   <u>Bats</u> have big <u>ears</u>, furry <u>bodies</u> and <u>wings</u> like <u>leather</u>.
4.   They sleep in <u>caves</u> and <u>attics</u> during the <u>day</u>.
5.   <u>Hedgehogs</u> have thick <u>spines</u> covering their <u>backs</u>.
6.   Most <u>squirrels</u> have big, bushy <u>tails</u> and live in <u>trees</u>.

Exercise 1.5

Sentences will vary. The collective nouns are underlined:
1.   a <u>clutch</u> of chicks
2.   a <u>labour</u> of moles
3.   a <u>shoal</u> of fish
4.   a <u>squabble</u> of seagulls
5.   a <u>warren</u> of rabbits
6.   a <u>parade</u> of elephants

Exercise 1.6

1.   On the way home, David and his family stopped for lunch.
2.   When Lucy arrived in Bristol, she went shopping.
3.   'The train to Portsmouth is leaving in three minutes,' said the guard.
4.   Have you read any books by Roald Dahl?
5.   'We've been waiting for ages,' said Mum. 'Hurry up!'.
6.   'Will Mrs Jackson please come to reception,' said Elizabeth.

Exercise 1.7

1. On Friday we went swimming.
2. 'Would you like to visit Spain this year?' asked Leslie.
3. The crowd cheered as England scored a try against Scotland in the final minute.
4. Jane's teacher welcomed Mr and Mrs Smith into the classroom.
5. Queen Elizabeth lives in Buckingham Palace, in London.
6. 'In march,' said Loren, 'I am going to Switzerland for a skiing holiday.'

Exercise 1.8

1. fudge
2. hedge
3. dodge
4. smudge
5. badge
6. lodger

Exercise 1.9

Badger
Bat
Fox
Hedgehog
Mole
Mouse
Owl
Rabbit
Robin
Squirrel

e	t	n	d	r	z	a	t	o	h
	y	x	w	r	w	m	e	u	e
o	q	b	o	n	f	o	x	k	d
m	y	b	b	e	z	u	t	j	g
i	i	m	a	r	t	s	i	q	e
n	o	j	t	d	b	e	b	t	h
o	h	v	u	i	g	v	b	q	o
l	q	z	d	h	a	e	a	s	g
w	d	e	s	d	t	c	r	n	z
t	e	r	r	i	u	q	s	o	c

Chapter 2

Exercise 2.1

1. Answers may vary; a suggestion follows:
    Savitri's eyes may be 'like lotus flowers' because they are pretty and delicate.
2. Savitri's sarees were made of the very finest silks, and she was always covered in jewels.
3. Answers may refer to green parrots, spotted deer or buffalo.
4. Savitri longs to enter the jungle. Lines which show this are:
    'How she longed to throw off her fine clothes and join them.'
    'How she longed to fling off her leather sandals and feel more than the hard, white marble beneath her feet.'
5. She manages to enter the jungle by slipping away one afternoon, while her ayah was sleeping and the gardener was bent over his rose bushes. She runs through the palace gardens to the wall, where she finds a small wooden door and escapes.
6. Possible alternatives are:
    (a) *intricate:*   elaborate, complex
    (b) *shimmering:*   sparkling, iridescent
    (c) *solemn:*   sad, sombre, glum
    (d) *dense:*   thick, solid, impenetrable

Exercise 2.2

1. Rati Fyzee is the oldest of the speakers.
2. Building space on the ground is so limited in Mumbai because it is built on a small peninsula.
3. Suraj experiences so many power cuts during the summer in New Delhi because it gets very hot and everyone has their air-conditioners and fans working flat out. They have a huge diesel generator that provides electricity when there is a power cut but this often breaks down.
4. According to Suraj, the government should generate more electricity in the future by using solar energy, since they have so much sunshine in India.
5. Answers may vary. A suggestion follows:
    Bhupinder's family is too poor to afford a proper house, so he has to share a small room with his extended family. He says that life is very hard for them, and he hopes

that one day he will get a good job and be able to look after his parents properly. This suggests that he has a tougher life than the other speakers in the passage.

6.   (a) Fay Singh makes her living making travel arrangements for business executives.

(b) She is unusual because once it was assumed that women would stay at home and take care of the family. But now Fay Singh has a high-powered job and goes out to work everyday.

Exercise 2.4

1.   The princess wore <u>pretty</u> sarees made of <u>fine</u> silk.
2.   Savitri loved to watch the <u>spotted</u> deer as they sprang through the <u>dappled</u> shadows.
3.   Sometimes she saw a <u>small, solemn</u> boy herding <u>dusty</u> buffalo down to the river.
4.   The palace was surrounded by gardens with <u>intricate</u> flower beds and <u>shady</u> paths.
5.   Savitri ran up to the <u>high</u> walls and ran her fingers across the <u>ancient</u> stones.
6.   The jungle beyond the palace was <u>green</u> and <u>dense</u>.

Exercise 2.5

Answers may vary; some suggestions are:
1.   Rati describes Mumbai as a <u>jostling</u> city.
2.   Suraj's home can become <u>blistering</u> during the summer months.
3.   They have an <u>enormous</u> generator to provide electricity when there is a power cut.
4.   Life is <u>tough</u> for Bhupinda and his family.
5.   Princess Savitri lived in a <u>magnificent</u> palace.
6.   Savitri thought the jungle looked <u>thrilling</u>.

Exercise 2.6

Suddenly, there it was. Just a small, wooden door. The only thing that stood between her and the outside world. She pushed and it opened. For a few moments Savitri stood absolutely still, just gazing in wonder. There was the jungle not more than three paces away, green and dense and very, very wild.

Exercise 2.7

1. Malaysian
2. Australian
3. South African
4. Swiss
5. Scottish
6. Hungarian
7. Israeli
8. Pakistani
9. Kenyan
10. Irish

Exercise 2.8

1. Spain
2. Argentina
3. Sweden
4. Holland
5. Scotland
6. Chile
7. Zimbabwe
8. Iran
9. Norway
10. Wales

Chapter 3

Exercise 3.1

1. The first thing that happened to the children was they began growing tails and then growing fur.
2. I do not think the teachers like the mice because they stand on their desks and shout 'Get out, you filthy mice! Get out!'
3. There is a clear rhyming pattern to this poem: the lines rhyme in pairs, called rhyming couplets.
4. Answers may vary; a suggestion follows:
   The author uses these kinds of words to suggest that the witches have a strong accent. The effect of the words is that they cause me to read the poem in a strange accent, as if I were one of the witches myself.
5. Answers will vary. Look for thoughtful comments, showing a good understanding of the poem and some description inferred by the witches' actions and words.
6. Possible meanings are:
   (a) *guzzling:* scoffing, eating greedily
   (b) *galore:* in large numbers, in abundance
   (c) *demented:* mad, crazy, manic
   (d) *amuse:* occupy, entertain

Exercise 3.2

1. Sentences should include: 'spiders' webs', 'frog-spawn' or 'other weird ingredients from forests and wild places'.
2. Answers may refer to:
   • sending someone into a long, deep sleep;
   • opening a door in a solid rock;
   • carrying someone across the world in a flash;
   • making people and things invisible;
   or
   • performing impossible deeds; enchanting someone; changing something completely.
3. (a) You may still see a wishing well today in castles, gardens or shopping centres.
   (b) If you find one, you should throw a coin into the water, close your eyes and make a wish.

4.   A wish-bone is special because if two people break it in two, the person with the bigger part is entitled to make a wish.

5.   You can enter the Sky World by climbing a rope or a ladder hanging down from the clouds, or from a tree so tall that its highest branches are invisible.

6.   Answers will vary. Reward thoughtful answers that show evidence of reading and understanding the passage. Look for references to all three things: spells, wishes and magical worlds.

7.   Possible definitions are:

(a) *enchanting:*   casting a spell on, bewitching, charming,

(b) *cauldron:*   large pot used for boiling

(c) *realm:*   land, territory

(d) *furnishings:*   furniture, carpets, etc. (which fill a room)

Exercise 3.4

1.   The witches <u>cast</u> a spell on the children and <u>turned</u> then into mice.

2.   The teachers <u>stood</u> on the desks and <u>shouted</u>.

3.   One child <u>thought</u> he was <u>growing</u> fur.

4.   If you <u>see</u> a wishing well, <u>throw</u> a coin in.

5.   The fairies and dwarves <u>lived</u> deep underground.

6.   I <u>met</u> a dragon king and he <u>gave</u> me a wonderful gift.

Exercise 3.5

1.   The witches all shouted 'HOORAY!'

2.   The children turned into mice.

3.   Mice were running around the schoolroom floor.

4.   Touch the object of your spell or blow on it gently

5.   We broke the wish-bone and I made a wish.

6.   You can reach it by climbing a rope or a ladder hanging down from the clouds.

Exercise 3.6

1.   The witch danced. (✓)

2.   The cauldron (X)

3.   I cried. (✓)

4.   The dragon kings (X)
5.   lies deep below the ground. (X)
6.   give you a wonderful gift (X)

Exercise 3.7

<u>subject</u> *verb*
1.   <u>The witch</u> *waved* her wand.
2.   <u>The wizard</u> *stirred* the potion.
3.   <u>The mice</u> *scurried* away.
4.   <u>I</u> *threw* a coin in the wishing well.
5.   Deep underground <u>the fairies</u> *danced*.
6.   <u>A dragon</u> *flew* past my window.

Exercise 3.8

Answers may vary. Some suggestions are:
1.   table – *stable, fable*
2.   witch – *ditch, which*
3.   girl – *twirl, curl*
4.   run – *stun, fun*
5.   school – *tool, rule*
6.   book – *look, took*
7.   address – *mess, less*
8.   soil – *foil, toil*
9.   hour – *flower, power*
10.   game – *fame, same*

Exercise 3.9

part – heart
plain – train
swimming – brimming
small – fall
worry – hurry

treat – sweet
bough – cow
find – behind
eight – Kate
naught – sort

Chapter 4

Exercise 4.1

1.   According to the chart, the treasure was buried beneath a tall tree on Mizzenmast Hill.
2.   One of the pirates yelled when he saw a human skeleton lying at the foot of a tree.
3.   (a) When the pirates heard a strange voice singing, they thought it was 'Flint's ghost'.
      (b) Long John Silver calmed them down by calmly saying, 'It's only someone trying to scare us.'
4.   Long John suspected there was going to be trouble because a huge hole had already been dug at the foot of the tree, showing that someone had got there before and taken all of the treasure. He suspected that they may be lying in wait to ambush his team of pirates.
5.   It seems that Dr Livesey and Ben Gunn may have shot the pirates.
6.   Jim and his rescuers made sure the pirates would not follow them by knocking a hole out in one of the boats and then taking the other, leaving them with no way of sailing out to sea.
7.   Possible definitions are:
      (a) *chart:*   plan, map
      (b) *pirates:*   sea robbers, buccaneers
      (c) *skeleton:*   bare bones (of an animal or human)
      (d) *pistol:*   fire-arm, gun

Exercise 4.2

1.   Answers may vary. A suggestion follows:
      I think the paper should be scrunched into a ball first to give the impression that the map is old and well-used. It will look like it has been handled many times.
2.   The land part is indicated by a line drawn around the island's perimeter. The sea is shown as waves outside the perimeter line.
3.   The writer suggests you could put lakes and volcanoes on your treasure island.
4.   Answers may vary. Possible words include:
      make, scrunch, flatten, dilute, paint, leave, dry, draw, add, shade
5.   Answers may vary. A suggestions follows:
      A map key is an explanation of what the symbols used on a map actually represent.

6.   Possible definitions are:
        (a) *scrunch:*   crumple, crush, squeeze together
        (b) *dilute:*   weaken by adding water, reduce strength by mixing with water
        (c) *outline:*   outside edge, perimeter
        (d) *symbols:*   signs, diagrams, drawings

Exercise 4.4

1.   'We'll be rich!' cried the girls, as they began to dig for treasure.
2.   'Do you think this island feels spooky?' said David.
3.   'There's treasure in my garden,' declared little Edward.
4.   'Land ahoy!' cried the sailor.
5.   Mary smiled and said 'When I'm older I'm going to be a pirate.'

Exercise 4.5

1.   The pirates asked 'Where is the treasure?'
2.   'Look what you've done to my boat!' shouted Long John Silver.
3.   'I'm glad you rescued me,' said Jim.
4.   'Why did you join the pirates?' Dr Livesey enquired.
5.   Ben Gunn said 'I know where the treasure is.'

Exercise 4.6

1.   At the end of the road <u>turn</u> right.
2.   <u>Whisk</u> the egg whites until they become light and fluffy.
3.   <u>Place</u> the cake on a baking tray and cook for forty minutes.
4.   To make the map, <u>draw</u> the shape of an island in the middle of the paper.
5.   After the church, <u>take</u> the second road on the right.
6.   To find the treasure, <u>walk</u> twenty paces east and then five paces west.

Exercise 4.7

Answers will vary. Look for the correct use of each word as an imperative verb to command, invite or instruct the reader.

Exercise 4.8

1. We tied a (knot) in the rope.

2. When I leave (school,) I should like to be a pilot.

3. The (lamb) was small and cuddly.

4. I saw a (sign) to London.

5. I found a splinter in my (thumb.)

6. The dog (gnawed) on his juicy bone.

Exercise 4.9

Sentences will vary. The silent letters to be underlined are:
1. glis<u>t</u>en
2. g<u>u</u>ine<u>a</u>-pig
3. w<u>h</u>y
4. tom<u>b</u>
5. <u>k</u>now
6. <u>w</u>rap

Chapter 5

Exercise 5.1

1. Answers will vary. Look for references to two of the following:
    *   a huge space
    *   important buildings
    *   grand statues
    *   many people
2. The first thing they had to stop for as they crossed the Forum was 'a fat snooty-looking senator… surrounded by his guards'.
3. The Temple of Vesta stands out so clearly due to the smoke curling up through a hole in its circular roof, from the sacred fire kept burning below to please the goddess.
4. The strong smell of incense made the writer's eyes water inside the temple.
5. It was a busy day in the Temple because it was the middle of the Vestalia Festival, with lots of respectable ladies visiting to pay homage to the goddess.
6. Answers will vary. Look for references to the girl's strong belief ('I know for sure') that a divine miracle occurred that day, because she asked the goddess Vesta for help.
7. Possible meanings are:
    (a) *divine:*   sacred, heavenly, godly
    (b) *forum:*   meeting place (often for discussion or debate)
    (c) *gawping:*   staring mindlessly, gaping
    (d) *sacred:*   holy, hallowed

Exercise 5.2

1. (a) The name the Romans gave to people who lived outside their empire was Barbarians.
    (b) They thought these people were uncivilised and violent.
2. Julius Caesar was killed in 44BC.
3. A centurion would lead 100 legionaries.
4. You might find markets, important public buildings and a wide open space in a forum.
5. Senator is the name for a member of Rome's leading council.

6.   Possible meanings are:
      (a) *uncivilised:*   rough, vulgar, uncultured
      (b) *invaded:*   entered by force, attacked
      (c) *governing:*   leading, controlling, ruling
      (d) *council:*   ruling body, committee

Exercise 5.4

Verb	First person		Third person	
	Singular	Plural	Singular	Plural
to laugh	I laugh	we laugh	he laughs	they laugh
to rise	I rise	we rise	she rises	they rise
to stay	I stay	we stay	he stays	they stay
to taste	I taste	we taste	he tastes	they taste
to dry	I dry	we dry	it dries	they dry
to care	I care	we care	she cares	they care
to catch	I catch	we catch	he catches	they catch

Exercise 5.5

1.   We enter the cinema.
2.   I dance on ice.
3.   I fall over.
4.   We eat chocolate cake.
5.   On a rainy day, I like to splash in puddles.
6.   After the match, we celebrate in style.

Exercise 5.6

1. Gregg said that <u>he</u> felt better now.
2. The players believed <u>they</u> could win the game.
3. Andie's parents said, '<u>We</u> would be delighted to come.'
4. 'Would <u>you</u> like to go fishing, Bevan?' asked Tom.
5. The queen drove past the crowds and gave <u>them</u> a wave.
6. Nikki and Petra said, 'Can you pick <u>us</u> up at five o'clock?'

Exercise 5.7

1. When Tim arrived at school, <u>he</u> realised he had forgotten his bag.
2. My parents told me, '<u>We</u> are very proud of you!'
3. Emma was delighted when <u>she</u> was given an A grade for her work.
4. Amil and Yoseph always shared jokes as <u>they</u> walked to school.
5. The aeroplane circled the airport for a few minutes before <u>it</u> landed.
6. Anzar asked, 'Would <u>you</u> like to go swimming on Saturday, Peter?'

Exercise 5.8

Alexandra
Andrew
Daphne
Edward
Elizabeth
Emily
Hassan
James
Joseph
Mark
Michael
Yolanda

Exercise 5.9

fire: state of burning, combustion
flask: long-necked bottle, pocket bottle
journey: travelling from one place to another, excursion
miracle: supernatural event, wonder
murmur: speak softly
sacred: holy, hallowed
secret: something hidden from others, private
statue: solid carved or cast image (of an animal or person)
temple: place of worship, shrine
tunic: close-fitting jacket, knee-length garment

Chapter 6

Exercise 6.1

1. The writer shares his room with four creatures.
2. The poet finds the spider's web curious; it is so fine he can hardly believe it does not end up tangled and knotted as he weaves and dangles on it.
3. Answers may vary. Look for reasons/evidence to support opinions – e.g. references to the idea that the poet sees the creatures as friends (good company for him).
4. Answers will vary. Look for more than the odd word or two, but sentences that describe the way the poem makes them feel, and lines or words which are particularly emotive for them. Reward answers that offer alternatives to the three words mentioned in the question (*friendly*, *cosy* and *scary*).
5. The poem follows a pattern of rhyming pairs (or couplets). Each pair of lines ends in a similar rhyming sound.
6. Possible meanings are:
   (a) *thread:*   fine cord, thin string
   (b) *curious:*   inquisitive, eager to know, questioning
   (c) *weave:*   form into texture by interlacing
   (d) *dangles:*   hangs loosely, suspends and sways

Exercise 6.2

1. Scientists have found nearly 400,000 different species of beetle so far.
2. (a) Beetles' hardened forewings are their most important feature.
   (b) These forewings fit over their hindwings like a case. This enables them to clamber about in all kinds of places to search for food without damaging their hindwings.
3. On Goliath beetles these hardened forewings are called *elytra*.
4. The scarab beetle glistens like gold.
5. Some smaller beetles put predators off from eating them by having bright stripes or spots on their bodies, warning other creatures that they are dangerous (or poisonous) to eat.
6. You would not want a scavenging beetle indoors because they can sometimes eat stored food.

7.   Possible meanings are:
        (a) *visible:*   able to be seen
        (b) *hardened:*   tough, strengthened
        (c) *delicate:*   fragile, easily broken
        (d) *predators:*   animals that hunt and kill other animals for food

Exercise 6.4

1.   What is the weather like in Spain?
2.   Mum shouted, 'Get down from there!'
3.   Kick-off will be at three o'clock.
4.   Mrs Jackson smiled and said, 'What a beautiful painting!' (or a full stop)
5.   Would you like mashed potatoes or chips?
6.   The train leaves in twenty minutes.

Exercise 6.5

Answers will vary.

Exercise 6.6

Answers will vary.

Exercise 6.7

Answers will vary.

Exercise 6.8

1.   foxes
2.   snakes
3.   maps
4.   matches
5.   loaves
6.   journeys
7.   tomatoes

Exercise 6.9

1. chart
2. country
3. lunch
4. cake
5. valley
6. flea
7. princess

Chapter 7

Exercise 7.1

1. (a) At the beginning of the passage, Augustus Gloop's mother is worried because her son is leaning too close to the river of melted chocolate.
   (b) Willy Wonka is worried because if Augustus falls in he will dirty the chocolate, which must remain untouched by human hands.
2. It is worrying that Augustus Gloop has a cold because he might pass it on to 'about a million people all over the country' if he infects the chocolate.
3. The line which tells me this is: '(Augustus *shrieks as he falls in*)'. You may decide to accept alternative lines, including:
   'Save him! He'll drown! He can't swim a yard! Save him! Save him!'
4. The first thing Augustus says as he falls in is 'Help! Help! Fish me out!'
5. Augustus has disappeared up a pipe (to a room where strawberry fudge is made).
6. According to the Oompa-Loompas, Augustus will be turned into a piece of fudge.
7. Possible definitions are:
   (a) *shrieks:*   yelps, screams, screeches
   (b) *delicious:* appetizing, very tasty
   (c) *colossal:*   huge, gigantic
   (d) *gorge:*   stuff yourself, eat greedily

Exercise 7.2

1. The fudge cakes take 80 minutes (1 hour 20 minutes) to produce in total.
2. You need 150g of butter or margarine in total.
3. You should mix the flour with the bicarbonate of soda.
4. You know that the cake mixture is cooked when it springs back when lightly pressed.
5. Answers will vary; include any two of the following:
   line, grease, preheat, place, heat, stir, cream, beat, sift, add, whisk, fold, turn, pour, allow, cut.
6. Possible meanings are:
   (a) *recipe:*   instructions for cooking/making something
   (b) *grease:*   lubricate, smear with oil or fat
   (c) *preheat:* heat an oven before placing food in it
   (d) *sift:*   put through a sieve

Exercise 7.4

1.   For this recipe I need garlic, tomatoes, onions and peppers.
2.   Will Julie, David, Greta and Paul please see me at breaktime.
3.   During our holiday we went surfing, fishing, riding and sailing.
4.   Our concert tour takes in Manchester, Birmingham, Bristol, Cardiff and London.
5.   I can play the clarinet, trumpet, piano and saxophone.

Exercise 7.5

1.   To make the model you will need pencils, glue, paper and scissors.
2.   The Headmaster would like to see Smith, Harrison, Jenkins, Patel and Thorpe at lunchtime.
3.   In the Autumn term the school offers soccer, rugby, netball, hockey and basketball.
4.   'This train will be calling at Reading, Swindon, Bath and Bristol.'
5.   I have invited Jake, Emma, Jemima, Lydia and Darren to my party on Saturday.
6.   On holiday we rode, swam, walked and ate.
7.   Our large, brown and friendly dog came too.

Exercise 7.6

1.   we're – we are
2.   you'll – you will
3.   I'd – I would (or I had)
4.   they've – they have
5.   I can't – I cannot
6.   we wouldn't – we would not

Exercise 7.7

1.   I should not – I shouldn't
2.   you will not – you won't (or you'll not)
3.   you have – you've
4.   we are not – we aren't (or we're not)
5.   she will – she'll
6.   he had – he'd

Exercise 7.8

Answers will vary.

Exercise 7.9

1. tangle
2. single
3. meddle
4. stumble
5. candle
6. rectangle

Chapter 8

Exercise 8.1

1. Accept: *barking* and *barked* (you may/not decide that *paws* or *tail* are not specific to a dog).
2. It was dangerous at this time because the ice was breaking up and thawing, so it was unsafe to walk on.
3. The lump of coal came from the bridge, when someone threw it over.
4. The ice made a growling sound as it broke up.
5. Clay and Hal managed to keep their hands warm as they crawled across the ice by resting their hands on their coat cuffs.
6. Possible meanings are:
   (a) *ventured:*   risked moving, bravely entered
   (b) *fissure:*   crack, split
   (c) *marooned:*   isolated, stranded
   (d) *sorrowful:*   unhappy, mournful, sad

Exercise 8.2

1. (a) The whale weighs seven tonnes.
   (b) It is 5m in length.
2. You would normally expect to find a bottle-nosed whale in the deep seas of the North Atlantic.
3. The whale injured itself by crashing into an empty boat.
4. Answers may vary. A suggested answer follows:
   Whales are difficult animals to help once they become lost because of their size and bulk. Redirecting them, or lifting them, would be very difficult indeed.
5. Alison Shaw is so concerned because if the whale were to swim upstream it would encounter more shallow, rocky waters, which would prove very dangerous for it.
6. 'relatively mature'
7. Possible meanings are:
   (a) *commuter:*   person who travels to work daily
   (b) *murky:*   clouded with dirt/silt; gloomy
   (c) *baffled:*   bewildered, perplexed
   (d) *disorientated:* lost a sense of direction, dazed and confused

Exercise 8.4

1. The ice begins to crack and break up.
2. Clay says 'We have to help rescue the dog.'
3. Hal and Clay crawl across the ice.
4. The crowds watch the whale in the Thames.
5. The whale is a long way from home.

Exercise 8.5

1. The dog was unhappy.
2. The children feel scared on the ice.
3. The whale is a long way from home.
4. Vets are remaining on standby.
5. The rescuers say it is the first whale they have seen in the Thames.

Exercise 8.6

1. On Saturday we went horse riding and then we went swimming.
2. Jeremy wanted to join us but he could not come.
3. Are you comfortable or would you like an extra pillow?
4. I like dogs but I prefer cats.
5. The winning team marched off the field and the crowd cheered as they left.
6. We could cook a meal at home or we could visit a restaurant tonight.

Exercise 8.7

1. Would you like some more apple pie or have you enough?
2. Sophia wanted to play outside but it was pouring with rain.
3. We spent two weeks in Australia and then we flew to New Zealand.
4. Mikey washed the dishes and his mother dried them.
5. I tried to get a table in your favourite restaurant but it was fully booked.
6. Will you come here or shall I come round to you?

Exercise 8.8

quarter
quite
quest
question
quack
liquor
quiet
cheque
quick
conquer

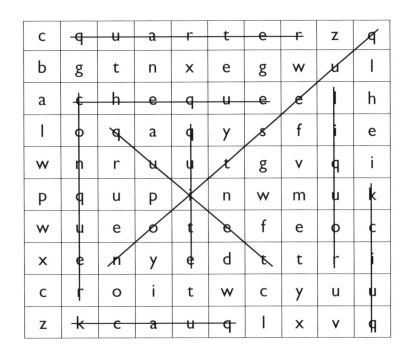

c	q	u	a	r	t	e	r	z	q
b	g	t	n	x	e	g	w	u	l
a	c	h	e	q	u	e	e	l	h
l	o	q	a	q	y	s	f	i	e
w	n	r	u	u	t	g	v	q	i
p	q	u	p		n	w	m	u	k
w	u	e	o	t	e	f	e	o	c
x	e	n	y	e	d	t	t	r	i
c	r	o	i	t	w	c	y	u	u
z	k	c	a	u	q	l	x	v	q

Exercise 8.9

Answers will vary. Check for correct spelling as well as meaning.

Chapter 9

Exercise 9.1

1.   The speaker's room was light when he woke in the middle of the night.
2.   After he got out of bed, he went to the window.
3.   'While the household quietly slept'.
4.   The garden looked so different because it was glimmering in a silver glow from the moon.
5.   The last verse reminds us of the first because it talks of imagined monsters once again and of returning back to bed.
6.   Each verse (or stanza) consists of two rhyming couplets (or pairs).
7.   Possible meanings are:
    (a) *household:*   family members sharing the same home
    (b) *peek:*   sneak a quick look, peep
    (c) *homely:*   familiar, comfortable, ordinary
    (d) *banished:*   driven away, made to disappear

Exercise 9.2

1.   Neil Armstrong was (/is) American.
2.   The astronauts' space capsule was called Apollo 11.
3.   It took Armstrong and his crew four days to reach the moon
4.   (a) The first thing Armstrong said was, 'The Eagle has landed.'
    (b) The people in Mission Control reacted to this news with a huge sigh of relief, replying 'We're breathing again. Thanks a lot.'
5.   The people on Earth were able to watch Armstrong's first steps on the Moon as he had taken a television camera with him.
6.   Possible meanings are:
    (a) *milestone:*   landmark, important event
    (b) *mission:*   operation, assignment (space)
    (c) *descent:*   journey downwards, fall
    (d) *historic:*   noted in history

Exercise 9.4

1.   The poet crept <u>silently</u> towards the window.
2.   <u>Excitedly</u> he gazed up at the silvery Moon.
3.   The Moon was shining <u>outside</u>.
4.   The crew at Mission Control watched <u>nervously</u> as Armstrong stepped out of the lunar module.
5.   Back on Earth, millions of people waited <u>patiently</u> for news of the mission.
6.   The families of the astronauts hoped their loved ones would return <u>soon</u>.

Exercise 9.5

Answers will vary.

Exercise 9.6

1.   They walked <u>beside</u> the river bank.
2.   Michael and Janet played <u>on</u> the tennis court.
3.   The flowers were placed <u>in</u> a vase.
4.   There were lots of presents <u>under</u> the tree.
5.   The letters came <u>through</u> the letter-box.
6.   I found an old football <u>behind</u> the fence.

Exercise 9.7

1.   I felt over the Moon when I won the competition.
2.   The children were hiding beneath the table.
3.   The train blew its whistle as it passed through the tunnel.
4.   The aeroplane climbed towards the sun.
5.   Jake walked along the path beside the canal. (or near)
6.   The tractor was kept in the barn near the old stable. (or beside)

Exercise 9.8

football
footpath
tablecloth
bookmark
bookshelf
goalkeeper
toothbrush
toothpaste
teapot
teaset

Exercise 9.9

Answers will vary.

Chapter 10

Exercise 10.1

1. Bertie often saw warthogs under the shade of the shingayi trees.
2. The arrival of a pride of lions would make the impala and the zebra flee the waterhole from time to time.
3. Bertie managed to find a better viewpoint from the high branches of a tree next to the farmhouse.
4. Answers will vary. Look for references to the black mambas, hyenas and vultures mentioned in the passage.
5. Answers will vary. Look for references to Bertie's love of lions and his constant wait to get a glimpse of them from his vantage point high up in the tree.
6. Possible meanings are:
   (a) *browsing:*   looking (in a casual manner)
   (b) *haven:*   safe place
   (c) *yearned:*   longed, desired
   (d) *forbidden:*   not allowed, prohibited

Exercise 10.2

1. This is unusual because most big cats live alone.
2. Many lion cubs die young because there are few scraps of food left for them after the male and female lions have eaten first.
3. Male lions defend a pride's territory by (any two of the following): spraying its borders with urine, roaring loudly at dawn and dusk, and attacking other lions who dare to appear.
4. Lions may also be found in the wild in India.
5. Both lions and tigers can kill animals larger than themselves.
6. Possible meanings are:
   (a) *related:*   associated, connected (e.g. by family)
   (b) *territory:*   region, geographical area (e.g. 'belonging' to a pride of lions)
   (c) *borders:*   edges/perimeter of a territory
   (d) *dusk:*   darker stage of twilight, partial darkness

Exercise 10.4

1. I sailed
2. it happened
3. you greeted
4. we laughed
5. she used
6. they watched
7. it rained
8. I kicked
9. you waited
10. he listened

Exercise 10.5

Verb	Present tense	Past tense	Future tense
to sew	I sew	I sewed	I shall sew
to wash	he washes	he washed	he will wash
to listen	you listen	you listened	you will listen
to grin	they grin	they grinned	they will grin
to march	we march	we marched	we shall march

Exercise 10.6

1. Mary had never been swimming before.
2. I do not want any more supper, thank you.
3. We are getting nowhere Let's start again.
4. I know nothing about the crime.
5. No-one has seen the cat since yesterday lunchtime.

Exercise 10.7

1. 'I have done nothing wrong!' protested the boy.
   or 'I haven't done anything wrong!' protested the boy.
2. 'I can't do anything for you until Tuesday,' said the plumber.
3. 'I didn't have any breakfast this morning,' said Mike, hungrily.
4. 'I won't ever do it again,' said Peter.
   or 'I will never do it again,' said Peter.
5. 'There are no spaces in the car park,' said Dad.
   or 'There aren't any spaces in the car park,' said Dad.

Exercise 10.8

1. 'Brilliant! I've won the competition for the third time!' boasted Nigel.
2. 'Excuse me, is the library open this evening?' Miss Jackson enquired.
3. 'Please can I have some pudding – I'm starving!' begged Timothy, greedily.
4. 'But I don't want to go shopping,' Julie moaned.
5. 'You always lose your glasses, Dad!' teased Paulo.

Exercise 10.9

Answers will vary. Reward accurate spelling and appropriate use of meaning.